Dedication

For my Mum, Sheila Robertson for giving me the greatest gift of all ~~~~~~ ~~ ~~~~ love of creativity

About the Author Moira Neal...

I learnt to machine sew when I was seven and have always had a love of making and creating. In the 1980's my husband Tony and I had a machine knitting business Tiny Tiger. You may remember seeing my hand framed squeaky and flashing knitwear in lovely little boutique shops and large outlets including Harrods, Harvey Nichols and Fenwick. The General Trading Company (GTC) in Sloane Square was our best outlet and sold huge numbers of our 'frog prince' sweatshirts which came complete with squeaker and flashing eyes.

The pinnacle of my career was hearing from GTC that they'd had an order from the palace for them for the two little princes!

As time went by I fulfilled my desire to be a nurse and trained at the age of 37 in 1990 having sold the business. After I had trained, I nursed part time and carried on being creative the rest of the time. I wrote four books on salt dough modelling, glass painting (2) and china painting as well as several hundred magazine articles for Popular Crafts on a plethora of different crafts and Crafts for Children using my first born granddaughter Hope as the model!

I studied patchwork and quilting City and Guilds part one and two which gave me a great grounding and the excuse for creative play. I have learnt that you do not have to stick to rules, whatever anyone tells you. As long as you enjoy what you are doing and feel happy in the process, that is enough. Finished is better than perfect. Once a project is complete you can move on to the next and immerse yourself in the enjoyment of creating another work of art purely for the fun of it!

I love to share ideas and help others get as much fun out of making and creating as I do. So it is with this book and all the wall hangings I am working on at the moment. I want people to laugh at my work and in the past two years it has taken on a lot more humour as you will see from future books.

Have fun...play...experiment!

I'm living the dream with my sewing machine

3

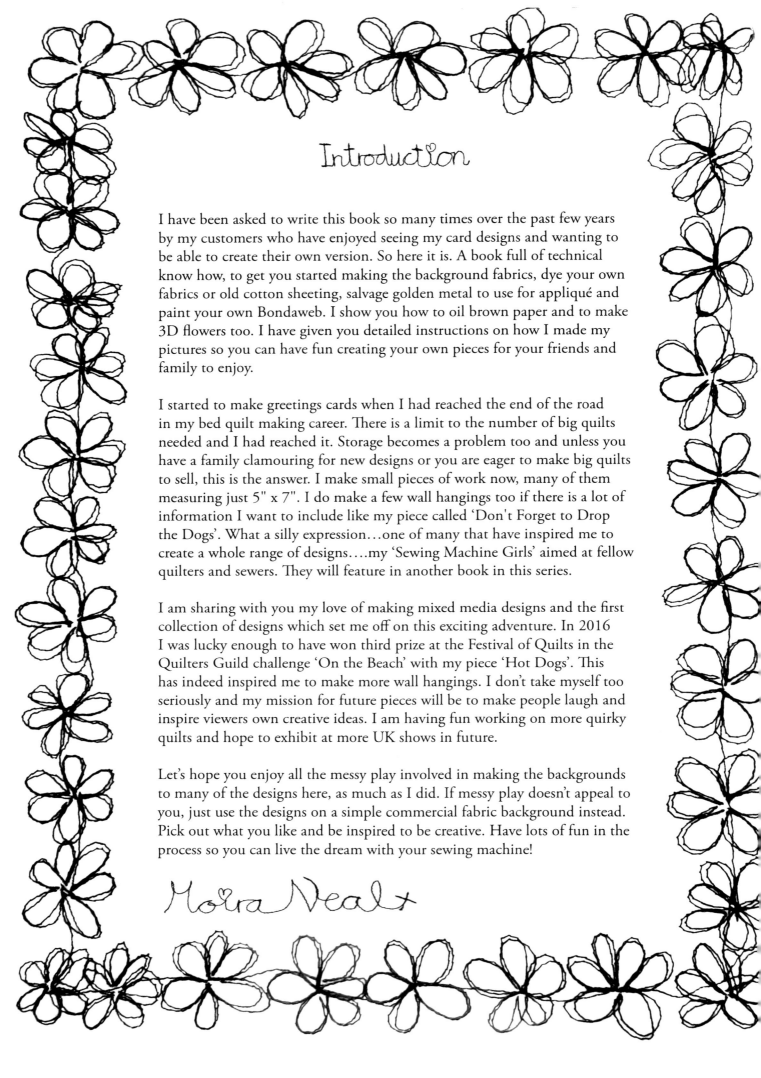

Introduction

I have been asked to write this book so many times over the past few years by my customers who have enjoyed seeing my card designs and wanting to be able to create their own version. So here it is. A book full of technical know how, to get you started making the background fabrics, dye your own fabrics or old cotton sheeting, salvage golden metal to use for appliqué and paint your own Bondaweb. I show you how to oil brown paper and to make 3D flowers too. I have given you detailed instructions on how I made my pictures so you can have fun creating your own pieces for your friends and family to enjoy.

I started to make greetings cards when I had reached the end of the road in my bed quilt making career. There is a limit to the number of big quilts needed and I had reached it. Storage becomes a problem too and unless you have a family clamouring for new designs or you are eager to make big quilts to sell, this is the answer. I make small pieces of work now, many of them measuring just 5" x 7". I do make a few wall hangings too if there is a lot of information I want to include like my piece called 'Don't Forget to Drop the Dogs'. What a silly expression…one of many that have inspired me to create a whole range of designs….my 'Sewing Machine Girls' aimed at fellow quilters and sewers. They will feature in another book in this series.

I am sharing with you my love of making mixed media designs and the first collection of designs which set me off on this exciting adventure. In 2016 I was lucky enough to have won third prize at the Festival of Quilts in the Quilters Guild challenge 'On the Beach' with my piece 'Hot Dogs'. This has indeed inspired me to make more wall hangings. I don't take myself too seriously and my mission for future pieces will be to make people laugh and inspire viewers own creative ideas. I am having fun working on more quirky quilts and hope to exhibit at more UK shows in future.

Let's hope you enjoy all the messy play involved in making the backgrounds to many of the designs here, as much as I did. If messy play doesn't appeal to you, just use the designs on a simple commercial fabric background instead. Pick out what you like and be inspired to be creative. Have lots of fun in the process so you can live the dream with your sewing machine!

Moira Neal x

You will need...

Plenty of old white cotton sheets!

Procion dyes or microwave dyes

Acrylic or fabric paints and brushes

Cotton wool roll

Wallpaper paste. Preferably one that does not contain fungicide

Tissue paper; old and crinkled is perfect

PVA glue

1", 2" and 3" brushes

Plastic sheeting for messy play

Baby wipes to keep your fingers clean

A BIG apron...one that covers most of you to keep your clothes clean!

Tomato puree tubes....start thinking about weekly menus to include chilli con carne and spaghetti bolognese on a regular basis and always buy your tomato puree in tubes not tins

Photocopies of interesting things like hand written recipes, children's poetry or stories and birth or marriage certificates

And finally.....when you have made the backgrounds you will need....

A sewing machine and darning or free motion foot. You need to be able to lower or cover the feed dogs to free machine stitch

Lots of black thread

Plenty of machine needles. I use old ones for working on unfriendly surfaces. I have been known to break five in one day

Curved scissors are a great addition to your work box

Bondaweb or other heat fusible web

Craft Vilene

An iron and board

Silicone sheets for protecting your iron and board from glue and paint

The most important thing you are going to need is

TIME,

a sense of humour and a

tolerant partner if you do not live alone! Things are going to get messy.....

5

Getting Started

As I sell my cards, I rarely use commercial fabrics in them. Most of what you see has been hand dyed by me. I love charity shops and always take the opportunity to buy up old cotton sheets as they take the dye so beautifully. They have a gentle softness and feel to them as well. Even the very thin, worn areas can be used for making backings. I waste very little and this worn out sheet is perfect for making paper fabric and cotton wool fabric.

Paper Fabric

I was inspired by Beryl Taylor's book. She makes hers on fine muslin... I use old cotton sheets. The advantage of making these backgrounds is that they are stable enough to allow you to free machine appliqué them without having to worry about layering up with wadding and backing as traditionally used in quilt making.

Warning!

This paper can lead to many needles getting broken as you do tend to get thick crunchy areas but the texture is fab and well worth it.

Above is a detail of some of the paper I used in making the boat design on page 33 and showing my Dad's signature and the date.

Before you begin, cover your worktop or table with a PVC cloth or polythene. Make sure you wear an apron to protect your clothes and fine rubber gloves if your hands are sensitive. Wash out all brushes well after using them for PVA glue as it will quickly ruin them if you forget! It is a good idea to have wet wipes to hand as well as jam jars for water and mixing plates for colours.

You will need

Old cotton sheeting torn into manageable pieces. I suggest starting with A3 size or smaller. PVA glue diluted about 50/50 with water. I make it up and keep it in a large jar so it can be shaken to mix it and used straight from the jar.

Method

Lay a piece of old sheeting out flat and paint the whole area liberally with the diluted PVA glue using a large flat brush.

Brush the back of the paper scraps you are adding and brush over the front to make them stick really well. Keep on adding the scraps of paper higgledy-piggledy all over the fabric. You can leave as much or little of the white background showing as you like.

Next, place the tissue paper over the top, leaving the wrinkles for extra texture. Slap on plenty of the PVA mix to make sure everything is well stuck down.

Dilute some paint and brush it over the top if you want to add some colour at this point. You can use watercolours, dyes or acrylic paints for this. See individual card designs for more details of how the backgrounds were produced.

If you want to stamp on any extra colour decide if you want to do it while the paper is still wet.

Leave until completely dry which will only be about 24 hours.

Peel the paper off the plastic sheeting and decide if you need to add any printing to it. You don't need anything fancy to do this. One of my favourite methods is to use a potato. If you have any small biscuit cutters you can push them into the potato to create a shape and cut away the excess with a knife. You can also make some great stamps using funky foam mounted on card or a plastic lid.

You can stamp over the paper fabric while it is still wet or leave it until it is dry. I like to keep my papers fairly simple and then add printing to suit the project I am working on.

Cotton Wool fabric

I was introduced to this messy play when I was doing my City and Guilds in Patchwork and Quilting with Annette Morgan. Much as I LOVE the look of it, this has to be the most hateful background to make. Wallpaper paste is slimy and very, very sticky and cotton wool is VERY attracted to it. It is worth making several pieces at once as the urge to do it again may not be with you again for a long, long time!

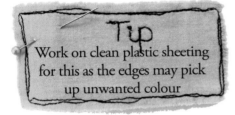

Tip
Work on clean plastic sheeting for this as the edges may pick up unwanted colour

You will need

Sheeting torn into the size you want. I like to keep mine quite small... up to A4. Cotton wool, separated into layers and just slightly larger than the sheeting. (You may need to butt pieces together.) Wallpaper paste, ideally without fungicide, made into the consistency of runny custard.

Method

Lay the cotton sheeting on the plastic cloth and slap the runny wallpaper paste all over it.

Pick up a layer of cotton wool and press it onto the cloth, patting it down well with your hands. Bare if you dare or not... you choose! Yes... by this stage I am shuddering with disgust as it is so difficult to stop the cotton wool sticking to my hands. Repeat the process of applying the paste and then another thin layer of cotton wool, making sure that you finish off with a coating of the paste.

When you feel the paper is thick enough, paint on or spritz with some diluted colour. You can use water colours or dilute dyes or well diluted acrylic paints.

Leave to dry which will take AGES! Even in the summer it can take three or four days for all the paste to dry out before you can peel off the sheets ready to use when creativity strikes.

I have a super collection of assorted colours to call on. I can stamp them with extra colour or words when I want to use them. You could transfer images onto them using one of the many methods available commercially. If you want the edges to look more rugged, you could hold the cotton wool

fabric over a candle and allow the edges to burn away slightly. Do this under an extractor fan or outside. Yvonne Brown uses this method in her lovely work.

Golden Metal

You can spend a lot of money on buying metal sheeting but it is much simpler to include chilli con carne and spaghetti bolognese in the family's meals as the tomato puree tubes hide a golden secret inside. The same is true for a certain canine toothpaste!

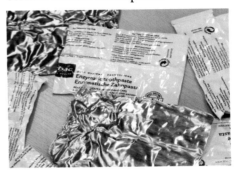

Warning! Metal tubes are very sharp when cut open so take care.

You will need

Empty metal tube, scissors, a blunt knife, an old wooden ruler or a boning tool and a foam mouse mat or piece of funky foam.

Method

Use scissors to cut off the top and bottom of the tube. Cut up one side too. Use the blunt knife to prise the metal open to reveal the golden interior. Wash it under the tap and then leave to dry.
Place the metal, golden side up on a flat surface and then rub hard with an old ruler or boning tool until the surface is completely flat. The metal can be embossed by placing it gold side down on a mouse mat or funky foam and drawing onto it using a blunt pencil or ball point pen. If you are going to use it for appliqué, you can iron Bondaweb onto the back.

3D Flowers

These flowers are quick and fun to make. I usually start off by sandwiching two layers of white cotton sheeting together with Bondaweb and then free machine flower shapes onto it. You could make this using two different dyed fabrics.

Now I do one of two things. If I want the flowers to be one colour I dampen the stitched piece and then spritz it with colour all over.

Leave it to dry and then cut out the flowers with really sharp, pointed little scissors. If you free machine them onto the background by stitching only the centres they will look 3D. See the card on page 21.

Here is another way of making them. This time I coloured each flower and leaf individually, adding a touch of yellow in the centre of each flower. This is the method I used for the Union Jack design on page 35. It is always handy to make a stash for use in future projects!

Oiled Brown Paper

It was the late Valerie Campbell Harding who introduced me to this fabulous surface while I was with her on a course at Belstead House. (Oh that wonderful place I hear so many of you sigh!)

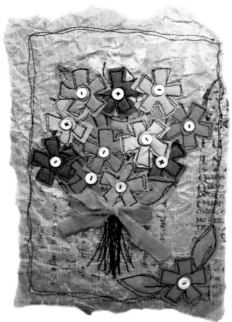

You will need

Brown paper & cooking oil. I used corn oil, a brush and a plastic bag.

Method

Scrunch up the paper and then open it out and brush it lightly all over with the oil.

Screw it up again and scrunch it about in the plastic bag to make sure the oil soaks in evenly all over the paper.

Open out the paper and leave it in a warm place to dry. I was amazed to find I could use it the following day. The secret is not to overdo the oil.

This paper can be printed before use. See individual designs for more information.

Brown paper fabric will need to be stabilised to free machine onto. For this I use craft Vilene and Bondaweb as follows.

Stabilising Fabric

Some fabrics and papers need a little more rigidity before they can be used for free machining onto and this is what I do.

You will need

Craft Vilene, Bondaweb (Wunder-Under) or any heat fusible web, iron and board and silicone paper.

Method

Cover the ironing board with silicone paper and have a second sheet to protect the iron. Cut the Bondaweb (and craft Vilene) to the size needed to back your fabric.

Lay the Bondaweb, web side (rough side) down onto the back of your fabric. Cover with the silicone sheet. Press with a hot, dry iron following manufacturer's instructions.

Leave to cool. (Speed this by laying it on a cold table top) Peel off the paper backing. You may need to scratch it with a pin first.

Place the craft Vilene onto the silicone surface, and align the bonded fabric over it. Cover and press. Leave to cool before use.

You could make these 3D flowers previously described, using the above method if you prefer.

Appliqué Fabrics

My favourite method of creating appliqué is to use Bondaweb. It serves two purposes... it is a great way of copying and transferring the design onto the back of the fabric and it stabilises and bonds the fabric too, making it easy to cut crisp shapes from it.

I have found over the years that I really dislike fiddling about bonding fabrics with Bondaweb so I have a big 'bonding' session in one go. I keep the bonded fabric in a large, flat, lidded container.

Pizza boxes would work well for smaller pieces. This method is perfect if you like to draw your design directly onto the back of the bonded fabric, as I do when I am creating new work.

Alternatively, trace or draw directly onto the paper backing of the Bondaweb, then cut the shape just outside the lines before bonding on the back of your chosen fabric. Cut out on the lines. Peel, iron to bond in place on your project and then sew round it in zig-zag, buttonhole or free machine stitch as I do.

Painted Bondaweb

I have always loved making painted Bondaweb backgrounds as it produces such incredible textures reminiscent of sand and sea. Sadly, it has changed recently and is not as well behaved as before and does not work as well but it is still worth experimenting with. There are different brands on the market so see which one works for you. Bondaweb has a 'nap'. It will wrinkle more one way than the other. Experiment and mark an arrow on the back to indicate the way it wrinkles.

You will need

Bondaweb cut to size. (It is worth painting several pieces at once in a selection of colours for future use) Four little pots to secure the corners of each piece of Bondaweb A 1" flat brush Acrylic paints or fabric paints. I like to use Golden liquid acrylics as they are so well pigmented. Although expensive they last forever and come in a great range of colours. Please note that watercolours and silk paints do not work for this. You will also need water, a mixing dish, and paper towels.

Method

Lay the Bondaweb rough side up. Mix the paint with water to make it a 'washy' consistency. Slap the paint on gently to avoid tearing the delicate web.

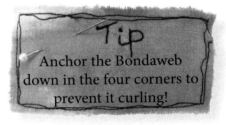

Tip
Anchor the Bondaweb down in the four corners to prevent it curling!

If you are using two or three colours it is worth allowing them to run together a little to get a watery look. Leave the web to dry flat.

The web can be used in several ways. If you want to create a stable background to stitch onto, simply cut some craft Vilene, fabric or paper fabric or cotton wool fabric to the same size.

Turn the web face down onto the background and use a hot iron to bond it, protecting the iron and board with silicone paper. Leave to cool completely before tearing off the silicone backing. It is very versatile and great to have a stash to hand in a selection of colours. Alternatively, cut or tear the web to the size or shape wanted.

When you appliqué fabric onto painted Bondaweb, cover it with silicone paper to avoid shininess.

Dyeing Fabrics

There is nothing I like more than a collection of hand dyed fabrics fluttering on the line! I use procion dyes as they have good light fastness. This is important if you are going to hang your work in a light room. If you are in a hurry and need a small quantity of fabric quickly, microwave dyes do their job in under ten minutes. I use Omega dyes for this and have a dedicated old microwave that is not used for food. It is fast and FUN!

Make sure that all utensils needed are kept separate. It is worth investing in a set of measuring spoons if you want to have repeatable success. I found some described as a drop, smidgen, pinch, dash and tad. They are precise measurements, starting from 1/32 of a teaspoon!

If you would like to do some traditional dyeing, buy a starter kit of dyes and chemicals and have a go. You can mix colours from magenta, turquoise, vivid lemon, golden yellow, scarlet and black. I use black plastic flower buckets from my local supermarket and I make sure I have my big dyeing sessions when Tony is not at home!

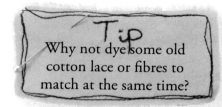

Tip
Why not dye some old cotton lace or fibres to match at the same time?

Microwave dyeing needs

Microwave dyes, salt, large glass bowl, cling film, measuring spoons, measuring jug, mixing spoon, microwave and washed cotton fabric or old cotton sheeting.

Method

Cut the fabric to the size you need and that will fit comfortably in the bowl.

Weigh it and record the weight for future reference. It is a good idea to keep a small book in which to record your successes and failures. Full instructions come with the dyes for quantities of dye to fabric weight ratio. Put a tablespoon or so of salt into the bowl, diluted with hot water. Add the dye solution and more water until it comes at least half way up the bowl. Mix well.

Open out the wet fabric and push it into the bowl using the spoon to move it around to take up the colour more evenly if that is what you want. Cover with cling film. Place in the microwave and cook on full power following manufacturer's instructions. Beware getting burnt from the steam which will escape from the cling film. Leave it in the oven to cool if you can. If not, use oven gloves and extreme care to remove it and tip the contents into the sink. Rinse with plenty of water until it runs clear, and then hang to dry.

Note: These instructions are for dyeing fabrics for use in picture

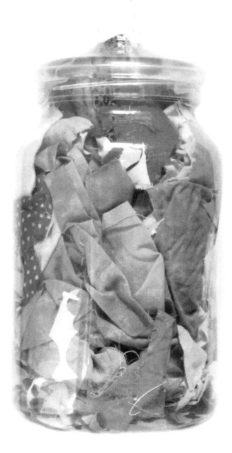

making only. Proper washing and rinsing will be needed if you are going to use dyed fabrics in quilt making.

Store dyed fabrics in a cupboard. Folded edges can fade in time if left out on display. I do keep all my off-cuts of fabrics in colour families in these big sweetie jars, but as they are constantly being pulled out and mixed about I don't have to worry about them fading.

It is great fun having a huge choice of colours to choose from. Enjoy making your own!

Scrappetti Fabric

This is such a useful fabric to make and I always have a stash of bonded sheets of assorted colours to use in my work. Separate your fabric scraps into colour families before you begin and then you can sit and chop up the fabrics when you have time!

Lay a piece of Bondaweb face up on a silicone sheet and then sprinkle liberally with your fabric bits. Cover with more silicone and press well. Leave until completely cold before taking a peek.

I like to store my sheets of scrappetti fabric in plastic ring binder sleeve or in a large flat box so I can simply tear off a piece as I need it. This is a great way to use all your colourful scraps to add texture to your designs or cut shapes from it. The more bits you have, the more variety of colours you can put together. I have used them on the Mum card page 29.

Tip

Save all your leftover scraps for making scrappetti fabric

Measure out dyes carefully with tiny measuring spoons for repeatable results!

Free machining

So here goes... just be brave and have some fun...Fit your machine with a free machine embroidery or darning foot. Lower the feed dogs or cover them, according to your machine instructions. Layer up your fabric with lightweight wadding, paper or craft Vilene to make it stable using safety pins or 505 spray glue, perfect for small projects, to keep the layers together.

Some people wear quilting gloves... thin gloves with a rubber coating but all I use are two pieces of rubber shelf matting 2" x 3" each. (see picture below)...They are just big enough to put under my middle three fingers. They give me the control and grip I need. Make sure they stay on the work, and keep your fingers close enough to the needle so you have control but at a safe distance. Stop sewing and move your fingers when you need to. Keep them safe; they are precious.

I always use the needle down position on my machine when I am free machining. If the phone rings, the needle stops firmly in the work. If you do not have that facility, always wind the wheel towards yourself to put the needle in the work if you want to stop and move your hands.

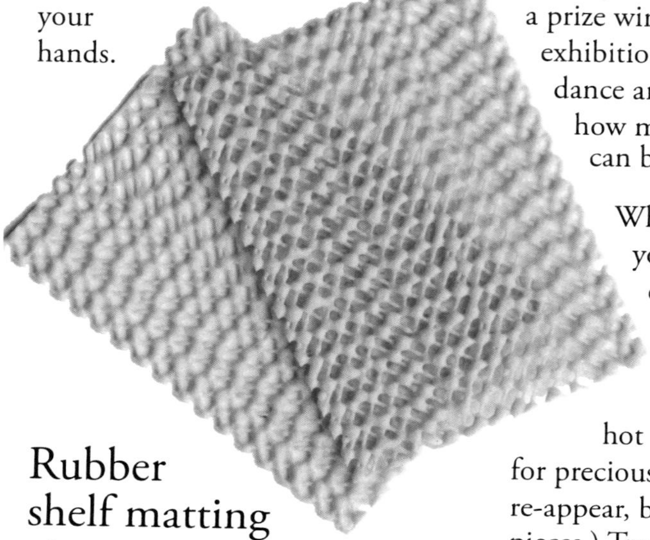

Rubber shelf matting gives you super grip!

Start simple. Be kind to yourself.

*Put the presser foot down. Let the machine take one stitch; pull up the lower thread to the surface. Put your foot on the pedal and simply push the fabric under the needle vaguely following the line. It doesn't matter if it looks awful... just go over it a few more times and it will look great, I promise. Next, add some bumps all around then try adding texture to the inside of the shape. Simply go where the needle takes you and enjoy the ride. * Some machines are happy to sew straight away without the need to pull up the lower thread. Experiment! The faster you move the fabric the faster you must sew.

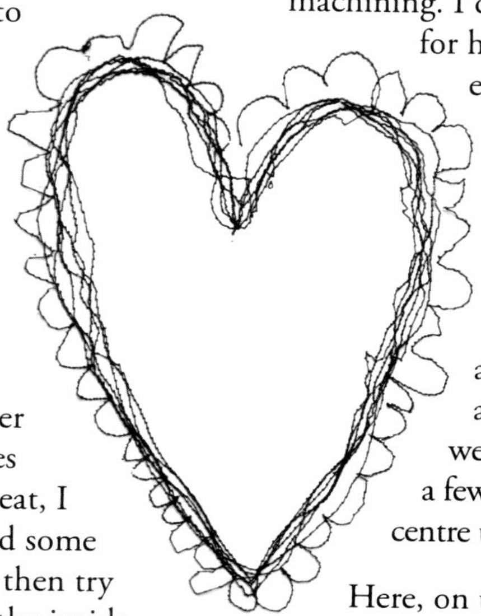

Once you have mastered the basics, be bold and try something more complex. It is fun drawing with the needle continuously. All lines look livelier if there are two crossing over each other. Deliberately re-trace your steps going near, but not directly on top of your previous line. Work fast and free....you are Creating Art and making a statement, not creating a prize winning quilt for the next exhibition. Simply enjoy the dance and you will be amazed at how much fun needle dancing can be!

When you are practising you can draw an outline on your fabric using a Frixion pen as it will disappear when you iron over it with a hot iron. (Not a good idea for precious projects as lines may re-appear, but great for practice pieces.) Try drawing a simple heart, flower or your own favourite shape

to use as a guide.

My granddaughter, seven year old Grace wanted to have a go at free machining. I drew a simple heart for her on paper and she enjoyed going around it but her first line was very wonky. I told her to just keep on going round and round and very soon it read 'heart'. I drew a second heart for her and once again she went round and round a few times then filled the centre up with squiggles.

Here, on this page is the third heart she stitched a few minutes later. I told her to add bumps all the way around the outside and this is the result!

The secret is to move and pause your hands as you draw just as you would with a pen. If you are drawing a point, you would make one upwards movement, pause, then a downwards movement. Try it with a pen and see if you understand what I mean. It is the same when you are free machining the bumps around the heart. Pause each time you touch the edge of the heart before allowing yourself to draw the next flowing curve, but let the machine keep sewing! It does not matter if you take two or three stitches on the spot. This way you will get a beautiful sharp point where the curve meets the outside of the heart.

Using this book

There are 17 card designs here to inspire you. There are no templates, but I have described how each was made. You can trace the outlines of the shapes onto the back of Bondaweb to create your own appliqué shapes remembering to reverse any text first. Change the colours, backgrounds and proportions and have fun making your own colourful versions for your friends and family.

Bring on the bling!

I love the sparkle of faceted sequins and have a lovely selection of them in my stash going right back to the early 1970's when I made all my own clothes (as most of us did back then!) I can remember rustling up a machine knitted tabard one day and then free machining it with gold and adding gold beads...in time for a party that evening. There were always far more beads and sequins than needed in the pack and so I am thrilled they can at last see the light of day again.

I always buy interesting sequins when I see them. It means I can audition them to find the best contenders for a project. Look out for them at quilt shows...you can never have too many.

To sew a sequin on, the simplest method is to use a tiny seed bead to secure it in place. For this you will need a beading needle...they are incredibly fine but are small enough to go through the tiniest of beads. Look at the photos...I start with a knotted double thread, pulled up from behind the work. (Use tiny stitches if you prefer!)

Push the needle through the back of the sequin and pull it down onto the work.

Add a tiny seed bead pulled down near the sequin... and then push the needle back through the sequin, directly under the bead. Secure with a few tiny stitches on the back of the work or simply push the needle up from behind to add another sequin next to it to add even more bling.

French knots are a really useful embroidery stitch to use alone or could be used to secure the sequins onto the work if you have no beads or you find your needle is not fine enough. Use two or three strands of embroidery thread for these.

Pull the thread up from the back.

Hold one end of the thread firmly while winding it around the needle two or three times.

Push the needle back down into the work, a minute distance away from the emerging thread.

Slide the knot down the needle onto the fabric as you push the needle through the fabric keep a tension on the thread until it has all been pulled though the knot. Repeat!

Pink Cupcake Stack

This is one of my first designs and it was incredibly successful as a greetings card. The actual size of it is 14" x 18" and it was worked on cotton wool fabric dyed while wet with pale pink and soft yellow. Once dry it was stamped using an old commercial foam stamp and gold paint.

If you would like to make your own version, think about the layout before you bond anything in place for this design. I made the cupcake stack first and then put the organza glass serving stand over the bottom edge of them to make them look as if they are sitting in the glass stand. Make sure that you leave enough room to add it.

Cut out the cup cake cases first but don't bond them in place just yet. The icing on the cupcakes is made from plain white cotton wool fabric. Tear it to a mound shape to 'fit' above the cases and use Bondaweb to fuse them in place on the background.

Next, appliqué the cup cake cases over them. Free machine the cakes using a different design for each one. Try doodling ideas with pencil and paper before you begin. I worked the cakes one row at a time so you can overlap the next layer of cakes slightly.

Bond a cherry shape on each one. Alternatively, if you leave this step until all the cakes are in position you could allow the cherries to overlap the cakes above, perhaps adding a couple of leaves too for extra colour.

Now you get to add bling and use some of your bead and sequin stash if, like me, you have bought them over the years because they look so pretty! Anchor each one in place using a seed bead. (See page 13 of the getting started section.)

If you don't have a bead stash you can use embroidery threads and sew a selection of embroidered flowers and French knots instead.

Bowl of Strawberries

This summery design was made as a card for Wilkin and Sons to sell in their lovely factory shop in Tiptree. They make wonderful preserves and the BEST lemon curd in the world!

The blue hand dyed fabric was screen printed using a design from an ancient book of illuminated lettering but you could use your own choice of backing for this. Support the fabric by bonding it on a base of craft Vilene or layer it up with wadding and backing.

Make a paper pattern for the glass container and use it to trace onto the back of Bondaweb. Iron it onto crystal organza and put to one side. If you then cut the template sides down slightly, you could draw around it onto the background so you have a placement line for the strawberries which are applied FIRST.

Cut out about ten strawberries and bond the first two in place using the bowl cut out as a guide to position them so they appear to be inside the bowl. Free machine them with short black lines to imitate seeds. Add more strawberries and machine them in place too.

Bond the bowl over them and free stitch around it as shown, adding the window light effect to make it look shiny. Layer up the last of the strawberries adding the details to them as you go.

Top the berries with a nice blob of torn plain white cotton wool fabric and machine around it before topping it with another strawberry and calyx and adding one in the foreground too.

Finally, hand sew a few clear glass beads in place to imitate sugar crystals.

QUOD
FUIT AB
INITI
+ + + +
QUOD AU
QUOD VI
OCULIS
QUOD
MUS, ET
NOSTRA
TRECTAV
DE
VERBO VITA

ET Vita manifesta
est vidimus, et tes
tamur et annunciamus
vobis vitam aeternam,
quae erat apud Patrem.

et apparuit nobis.
QUOD vidimus et
audivimus, annuncia
mus vobis, ut et vos
societatem habeatis no
biscum nos
tra
cum

te ambulamus
et veritat
vidimus

1

Button Bouquet

This design has been very popular. You could make yours in your own choice of colours and flower shapes using pretty commercial fabrics or tiny gingham checks.

Prepare a background from oiled brown paper bonded onto craft Vilene for rigidity as described on page 8 in the getting started section. I screen printed mine with vintage text and stamped it with gold flowers but you can use anything you like to decorate yours. Potato printing works very well!

Cut out eleven or so flowers from a selection of fabrics and several green leaves. The design was worked in layers by bonding leaves and flowers in place and then overlaying and stitching more in place as shown.

Have a 'dry run' first by laying the flowers and leaves in place and moving them around until you are pleased with it. If you take a picture before you dismantle it to start sewing, you will remember which flowers and leaves to add next.

Once you are happy with the arrangement, bond and free machine the flowers and leaves in layers. Cut all the threads before moving on to the next layer. Add plenty of stitched stems sewing fast and free.

Next, free machine all the way around the outside of the brown paper allowing the two lines to criss cross as you go to create a lively look. Add one flower and leaves in the corner.

Hand finish by adding a vintage mother of pearl button in the centre of each flower and add a strip of torn fabric to make a bow. I used a large needle to thread the fabric through the backing and tied it in place. Admire!

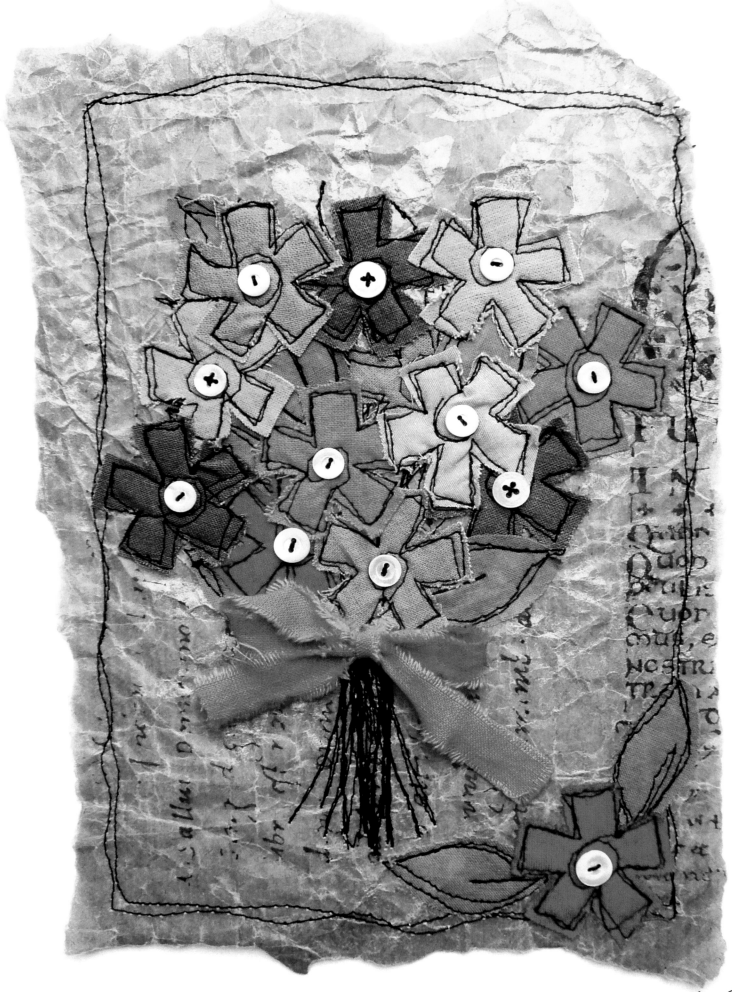

1S

Vase of Flowers

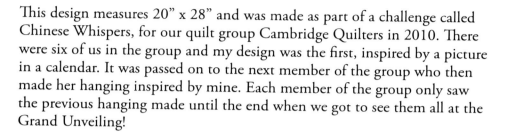

This design measures 20" x 28" and was made as part of a challenge called Chinese Whispers, for our quilt group Cambridge Quilters in 2010. There were six of us in the group and my design was the first, inspired by a picture in a calendar. It was passed on to the next member of the group who then made her hanging inspired by mine. Each member of the group only saw the previous hanging made until the end when we got to see them all at the Grand Unveiling!

The background of mine was made from old cotton sheeting which was painted with watery washes of green and blue fabric paint. It was overprinted with a selection of commercial stamps using acrylic or fabric paints.

I appliquéd the vase using hand dyed fabrics and over appliquéd with torn pieces of pale pink, dark pink and orange fabrics and two lines of black stitching. White lines were drawn on in a grid using a gel pen, but you could use line of white free machine stitching instead.

The flowers are both flat and 3D and cut from three shades of pink. The stems and leaves were all appliquéd flat although the 3D method can also be used for the leaves as in the Union Jack idea on page 35. Look closely at the picture to see how the stems, flowers and leaves were appliquéd in layers. All the 3D flowers were added last of all.

To make the 3D flowers, (and leaves if you wish) see page 8. Cut them out and apply them to the background with black free machined centres to anchor them in place.

Play around with the layout by having a 'dry run' before stitching the leaves and flowers down. Scatter a few 3D flowers in the front.

Floral Heart

The background is made from Bondaweb painted in pinks and mauves and then ironed onto craft Vilene. I so love having a stash of painted Bondaweb I can call on. Over the years I have found it very therapeutic to do when I've felt uncreative or life has been difficult to cope with. See page 9 of the getting started section for step by step instructions.

Always use silicone paper or those wonderful silicone baking sheets to protect your iron and board from the glue. Once the Bondaweb was ironed onto the backing it was over stamped in gold.

I used twenty one flowers, cut from my collection of hand dyed old cotton sheets to appliqué the heart shape. Dyeing is another favourite occupation and always so useful! Scale the flowers size up or down depending on the size of picture you want to make and use whatever colours you like from your stash or dye your own.

If you look closely, you will see that three of the flowers were added, along with the green leaves, after the first ones had been free machined in place. I love the layered look and find it the easiest way to create a natural looking design. Simply keep layering up as many flowers as you think the design needs, sewing one layer at a time.

Hand sew tiny seed beads in place in clusters of three to six beads but you could add French knots instead. See getting started section page 13.

23

Black Cat

My granddaughter Hope was in my studio a few years ago and suddenly announced... 'The black cat was so fat he sat on the mat wearing a hat!' I decided it would be fun to illustrate it for her so here is my version... 'he' became a 'she'. I invited Hope back to put the eyes in place as I wanted her to see how you can change the personality completely by moving them around. I love the expression she has captured and it has proved to be a very successful design.

I missed a friend's birthday a few days later so made another version of the card which read 'The black cat was really sad...she missed your birthday and that was bad!'

The background fabric was tray dyed, using turquoise, green and purple dyes, bonded then stabilised with craft Vilene. To make the picture, cut out the mat shape and then slash into the ends and fray them slightly. Bond the cat and mat in place.

Free machine around the cat with loose spiky movements to give the impression of fur using black thread. Look at the picture to see how I have stitched around the mat. I used straight stitch to create the stripes, moving the fabric back and forth.

Bond the hat in place and free machine it adding the flower as you go. I think it would be fun to add tiny appliqué flowers to her hat for a little extra colour.

Change to white thread and free machine the outline of her nose and mouth then use the picture to guide you to add whiskers and outline of her front legs and paws. I used stick-on gems for bling and cut the prongs from the back of safety cat eyes before glueing them in place.

Keep the hanging out of reach of small children if you use stick on embellishments as I have done.

Thanks

My original piece of work for this measures 10" x 7". Although mine says 'Thanks' you could put a name or other message or name on yours.
Stamp the background fabric using a texture stamp or make your own. I made mine from a lino print and this kind of textured design is really useful for backgrounds. You could make a similar design using a potato print by gouging lines in a large potato. If you do, make sure you print plenty of fabric with it in different colours to use in future projects before it goes off. I LOVE having a stash of fabrics to use when I am feeling creative!

Bond the dry, printed fabric onto craft Vilene to stabilise it for free machining or layer it up with wadding and a backing if you prefer.

Trace the letters, flowers, leaves and stems onto the Bondaweb backing (remember to reverse any letters you trace this way) and then iron them onto your choice of coloured fabric. Cut out the letters, position and bond them on the left side, then free machine around each one once or twice.

Cut out three rose shapes and appliqué each one separately, layering them up using the picture as a guide. I felt mine needed to be a little darker so I used a fabric marker pen to add a deeper colour. Appliqué the stems and leaves, overlapping the two lower roses with them.

Tear a strip of plain fabric for the tie and thread it through the background with a large needle and tie in front.

Hand sew a few stars in place using seed beads to anchor them as described on page 13.

27

Mum's the Word

Unusually for me I have used gold and pink threads in making this design! I photocopied an old sheet music book to make the pink paper fabric background. The pink colour was run into it while it was wet. Deeper pink flowers were stamped onto it later when it was dry. The original piece of work measures 11" x 15". See page 6.

The white layer of paper fabric was made with torn pages from an old technical building book and more of the sheet music scraps, lots of PVA glue and white tissue paper. You could use something more personal like copies of a marriage or birth certificate.

The word Mum was cut from scrappetti fabric (see getting started section page 11) made from three different shades of pink fabrics with some gold lurex to add some sparkle. The leaves were made from a selection of greens and gold lurex scrappetti fabric. Simply draw the shapes on the back of the bonded scrappetti, cut out and then carefully peel off the backing, cover with silicone paper or sheeting and iron in place before stitching.

I used gold thread to machine sew the letters in place. Sew slowly and use a denim needle or a metallic needle as they have a larger eye and can stop the thread from shredding. Be careful what metallic thread you buy. If it is too cheap it may well keep breaking.

I cut out the petals from Mum's hand made and dyed old lace but you can substitute commercial lace or fabric instead. Appliqué them with two or three rows of gold stitches.

Finally, add a smattering of sequins all held in place with seed beads. See getting started section for 'how to' on page 13.

Blue Campervan

I was really pleased with this design as I made myself learn how to create a collection of six different coloured vans using Adobe Photoshop to sell as cards when campervan cards were very fashionable. Mine were blue, red, purple, orange, yellow and green. I made one design with all six coloured vans on one card!

The starting point was a very plain paper fabric background made with plenty of PVA glue and tissue paper given a watercolour wash of green while it was still wet. See page 6.

Start by cutting out the body, door and window shapes and align them on the background laying the windows under the window frames. Cut the windows from crystal organza, and the trims from silver lurex. Add the windscreen wipers and the thin silver trim over the 'v' area, lights and the VW symbol. For information about appliqué see page 9.

For the indicator lights, trap a little orange fabric under organza, then add a ring of silver lurex. Make the headlamps by laying the organza over the background blue fabric and a ring of lurex on top.

Free machine around everything twice. Cut all the loose threads and then add the bumper and shiny lurex trim. Free machine around them and add the tyres in stitch. Finally, add the number plate with two wonky lines of stitch and free machine the word 2SURF or a personalised number plate. Add grasses in the foreground fast and free and flowers too if you want a more colourful design.

31

Boat

This card is very special to me. The background is made of paper fabric (page 6) using photocopies of the plans for the 'C' class canoe 'Clyde', that my dad Ian Robertson re-designed in 1948. If you look carefully at the picture you will see his signature along the right hand edge. The original piece measures just 6.25" x 4.5".

Dad died in 1965 when I was twelve years old but I was thrilled to get a copy of these plans about five years ago and have used them here. The paper fabric was given a watery wash of blue while it was still wet. Having his signature on the side of the card was accidental...it was a while before I noticed it, but it has given the card a special meaning for me.

The mast, flag, sails, and hull were all appliquéd at the same time. Looking closely at the picture I realise that I have added red fabric over the batten pockets in the sails to add more colour but not stitched over them. Oooops!!

The foamy sea wash was made from plain white cotton wool fabric, shown on page 7, and stitched around just once. You could personalise the sail by adding initials or numbers for a special birthday.

White iridescent sequins were anchored with glass beads, with some beads sewn on separately. Check out page 13 for details. Gosh...I remember buying them in the 1970's. I guess many of us have bought goodies over the years thinking they will come in useful one day...well that day has come!

33

Union Jack

Here the background is made from paper fabric shown on page 6. I photocopied a selection of old needlework bits and pieces like cards of buttons, snap fasteners and darning threads. I also included yellowed pages from a vintage paperback sewing book. You could use pieces of old paper pattern too. The paper was coloured with green and blue watercolours and stamped with gold acrylic paint when it was dry.

The flag shapes were made from strips of hand dyed sheeting. The pink and purple strips were torn, not cut to give a rough edge. I up-cycled my Mum's hand made lace, taken off old clothing, by dyeing it along with the pink fabric. I love to think that both our crafts have come together in this design. Mum only ever made white, black or ecru lace. As most of it was white, I chuck it into the dye pot with my sheeting so I always have co-ordinating lace and fabrics to use.

The flowers were made from two layers of fabric bonded together and then free machine stitched with flower and leaf shapes. The piece was then wetted, and diluted colour painted on and left to dry before cutting out. You could make them in the same way as the ones on the Vase of Flowers on page 21 using ready dyed or printed fabrics. See the getting started section on page 8 for how to make both types of 3D flowers.

I cut out the flowers and leaves and sewed them in place, with plenty of black stitching, anchoring the leaves along one end and the flowers in the centres to create a 3D look.

35

Beach Hut

The background was made from cotton wool fabric, shown on page 7, which was painted in yellows and blues once it was dry...oh how I wish it didn't take so long to dry! Allow areas of white to show through as you brush the paint onto it.

Cut out and bond the hut shape in place and then add the fascia board to it. Use a fabric marker to mark the door area. Free machine the vertical boards leaving the area for the door free as you go going over all the lines twice. Cut out and appliqué the door with one or two rows of stitch and then add the seagull on top of the roof.

Bond the grass shapes in front of the hut, and free machine them before adding the grey stones.

Cut out and bond the anchor in place. I used a scrap of rusted fabric for mine. Free machine around the stones and the anchor and add the grasses between the sand and sky on both sides of the hut.

Hand finish the picture by adding tiny fabric flowers anchored in place with seed beads. I used a brass paper fastener (brad) as a door knob and to hold the rusty anchor in place but a bead would do fine.

I cheated and printed out the words 'Anchors Away' on paper but you could free machine yours instead using any words that have a special meaning to you.

Anchors Away

Sheep on a Hill

Make a cotton wool fabric background, shown on page 7 for this design and give it a wash of pale blue while it is wet. You could leave white areas in the sky for clouds if you were making it specifically for this design. When I make up the backgrounds, I make a stack not knowing what will become of them. I LOVE being able to grab one and be creative with it without having to wait days for it to dry!

I used snippets of a really interesting green and black yarn for the hill. You could use torn strips of green fabric snipped up to make it look grassy. Free machine everything down with invisible thread or use a variegated green thread if you have one.

Cut the legs and face from black and bond the legs down. I like to free machine in layers and so I would machine them first before adding the sheep's body. The body is made from plain white cotton wool fabric and stitched with black thread to add a woolly texture and hold it down. Again, do this first before moving on.
Cut some short lengths of green wool for him to eat then bond the head in position over it. Free machine around it in black thread.

Hand sew on flowery sequins held down with white seed beads or use embroidery threads to add a few flowers. See page 13 of the getting started section.

Pengoo

When my nine year old granddaughter Grace came over one day she asked if she could make a penguin picture and here it is. When my son saw it a few weeks later he asked if it was a new card design, so it quickly became one! I added the gold crown. It became a very popular card design, often bought by fellow Grannies as inspiration for a project to teach their grandchildren to sew.

Children have no concept of free machining being difficult and no matter how wonky the lines might be, two wonky lines equals lively. I taught Grace to free machine on paper as it is stable and she very quickly worked out just how fast to move her hands and press the foot pedal to get the stitch size right. I put the foot pedal on an upturned waste paper basket as her little legs were too short to reach it on the floor.

Even now, when I teach free machining, I show Grace's first shaky efforts of stitching hearts on paper as they look lively, despite the wobbly stitches. You can see her third heart attempt on page 12.

This picture is worked on hand dyed fabric bonded onto craft Vilene. Grace cut out and bonded all the shapes onto it before she started to sew around it. You will see that the iceberg was stitched from the bottom, up around his feet and back down the other side. She sewed around the other areas with two lines of stitch. The catch lights in his eyes and beak were lightly painted with white acrylic paint using a dry brush.

The crown was sewn separately by 'Granny Moira' with gold lurex fabric onto pelmet vilene and then cut out and added as an afterthought. You could appliqué yours straight on if you wanted to give your version a crown.

If you are encouraging a child to sew, ask them what their favourite animal is...you might find yourself helping to create an elephant or a dinosaur or mouse.
Who knows?!

Beaded Cupcake

I made this design using a paper fabric background, shown on page 6, made from photocopies of photographs. It was washed with pale pink colour while wet. It was a long time after I had made it and had it printed out as a picture that I realised that in the background is a photocopy of my granddaughter! You can just make out her face and arm. Ah well...that is the fun of making your own papers...you use copies of pictures that you have and that have some meaning to you.

The icing for the cupcake was made with white cotton wool fabric. The case was cut from plain pink fabric and the whole lot was free machined in one go. Take a look at the Pink Cupcake Stack on page 15 for more ideas of free machined designs for the cupcake.

I appliquéd on the flower and then free machined a stem and leaves up to it, swirling the stitches around the flower centre. Next, I added three lines of wibbly-wobbly stitching around the sides. Just sew two lines if you prefer and maybe trap scraps of torn fabric into them as you go in the same way as the page borders on pages 18 and 20.

I decided that the design needed more colour as I'd not used green for the leaves so added bling by hand sewing the green beads over them. I decorated the icing with some holographic flowery sequins held down with seed beads. See getting started section on 'how to' page 13.

Interestingly, the actual size of this piece is only 5" x 7" hence my stitches look huge!

43

Seagull

The sea in this picture was made from painted Bondaweb (page 9) ironed onto craft Vilene. The sky was cut from pale blue hand dyed fabric and bonded above it. I cut the island from paper fabric, shown on page 6, painted grey with acrylic paint once it was dry.

The mound that the seagull is standing on was made from brown paper fabric and free machined before adding the gull, cut from one piece of paper fabric painted white and grey. His beak and legs were cut from orange painted paper fabric and I cut into his beak so he appears to be holding a fish cut from silver lurex.

I painted the rock with touches of white paint for the guano, added old orange veggie netting that I had sprayed with silver paint and wisps of cotton wool in the foreground. I even cheated and used cotton wool for clouds in the sky. Use white cotton wool fabric free machined stitched with invisible thread for a more permanent finish.

Hand sew a few glass beads onto the sea to add sparkle. Remember to add a couple of birds in the sky, either by appliquéing with white fabric or stitching them directly onto the blue sky.

Grace's Fairy

(Back page)

I used pink and green dyed cotton wool fabric for the basis of this design. It was lightly stamped with a commercial stamp once it was dry although the design is barely visible.

The gorgeous golden metal from the inside of a tube of tomato puree tube was up-cycled for her dress. This meant spaghetti bolognese again for dinner! Be warned: the metal is razor sharp so handle with great care. If you lay the dress and wings golden side down onto a mouse mat or a sheet of funky foam you can use a blunt pencil or ball point pen to emboss a design into them. See page 7 for more information.

I cut the fairy from pale pink fabric and appliquéd her arms over the wings. Her legs were added under the golden dress.

The organza flowers were cut using a hot tool. I used temporary spray glue to hold it firmly onto a sheet of mount board and then cut out each flower shape with the fine tip. A fine tipped soldering iron would work fine too.

The leftover piece of organza was free machine stitched onto the right hand side of the design using flowery shapes. The same linked flower design was stitched above her head as a garland. It was given a quick blast from a hot air gun to distress it slightly. The cotton wool fabric was not affected by the heat.

The organza flowers were hand sewn in place using a flowery sequin and seed bead by my then, four year old granddaughter Grace. Children love to be allowed to help. I used a blue fabric marker pen to make a dot on both the front and back of the piece so she could see where to push the needle through. I was impressed that she managed to sew on all three layers so accurately.

Have fun making your own version and embellishing with beads and sequins from your stash! Full details are on page 13.

Acknowledgements

I would like to thank all of you who have bought my cards, come to my home on free machining play days and told me this is the book you wanted me to write. Thank you for encouraging me to do it and to keep on making my cards. I would also like to thank my friends and family for their support and encouragement and to Tony for putting up with me and my mess! Once again a thank you to Jennie Rayment who said I could do the graphic design myself. This time I have learnt a new trick...wrapping text around an object. These little skills are so pleasing and I hope to learn a few more when I work on the next book.

A special thank you goes to Lindsey Freeman for proof reading. It is much appreciated.

I plan several other books in the series so keep a lookout for one on 'Making Faces', 'Sewing Machine Girls' and the one thing I love more than any... 'Free Machining'. I have recently discovered a love of India and have been inspired to create lots of Indian inspired free machining doodles which I hope to share with you one day. I just need time... in the meantime I plan on taking a break and I'm making a zany wall hanging... just because I can, now I am retired and the proud owner of a free bus pass!

If you have enjoyed this book, you may also like 'Colourful Canvas Landscapes' Free machine appliqué on painted canvas. ISBN 9780948160042, written in 2016 about how to paint and appliqué your own lovely landscapes onto canvas frames. Be warned...it is very addictive! It is available on Amazon.

Suppliers

Old white cotton sheets can be bought from charity shops Nationwide and car boot sales too. A great excuse (if you need one!) to go and enjoy finding things you didn't know you needed.

You may also be lucky enough to find jars of old buttons to use as embellishments. I support the local Salvation Army shop in my village and I'm also lucky enough to have friends who off load old cotton sheets from clearing out elderly relatives' homes. Just occasionally I am lucky enough to be given NEW vintage sheets. These I keep separate and wash them well before dyeing to use in projects that I hope will last a long time. Remember well used vintage cloth will already be weak and not stand the test of time.

Microwave dyes may be bought online from
Gail Smith at Omega Dyes
Belvedere Park
Bristol Road
Whitminster
Gloucestershire
GL2 7LU
Tel 01452 668857
email omegadyes@abigailcrafts.co.uk

Bondaweb, craft Vilene, procion dyes, paints, beads and sequins are available from
Colourcraft
Unit 5 and 6
555 Carlisle Street East
Sheffield
S4 8DT
01142 421431
www.colourcraftltd.com

47

'Grace's Fairy' worked on cotton wool fabric with golden tomato puree tubes, organza, beads and sequins. See page 46

ISBN 978-0-948160-05-9

The Fallen Angel Co

www.thefallenangelco.com